St Andrews in the 20s, 30s and 40

Helen Cook

A January morning in 1936 and James Cargill, his son Danny and fellow fisherman Sam Smart were returning to harbour in his boat, the Dundee registered *Bella and Betsy*, when the propeller shaft slipped and, with no sail, were immobilized 400 yards from shore in a stormy easterly sea. Their distress flare was spotted and David Fenton and the life boat crew were called out, as was Fred Warnes (1877-1962) the coastguard and commander of the Rocket Brigade, but the low tide prevented the launch of the life boat The trio rode out the storm until midday when Alex Martin's fishing boat the *New Sea Flower* towed them into harbour, watched by a large crowd.

St. Andrews

1 South Street	8 Bell Street
2 Abbey Street	9 St Mary's Place
3 Abbey Walk	10 City Road
4 Crail Road	11 Gibson Place
5 Bridge Street	12 Petheram Place
6 Largo Road	13 Strathtyrum Road
7 Argyle Street	14 North Street
	15 Market Street

A Castle ruins	C Cathedral ruins
D Tower of St. Regulus	E Town church
H Madras College	U University
F Blackfriars Monastery	

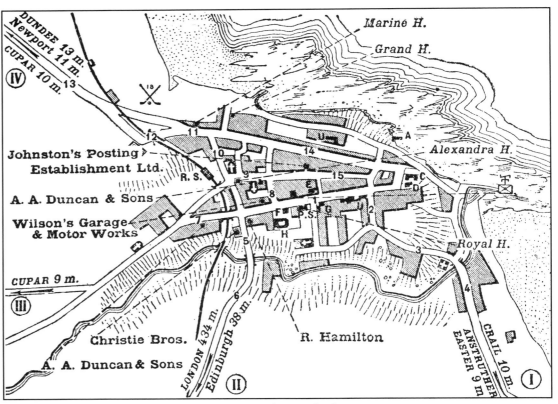

Further Reading

With the exception of *Old St Andrews*, none of the following titles are available from Stenlake Publishing.

Three Decades of Historical Notes, Ronald G Cant et al,
        compiled by Mary M Innes and Joan A Whelan, pub.
        St Andrews Preservation Trust, 1991.
Old St Andrews, Helen Cook, pub. Stenlake Publishing Ltd, 2001.
St Andrews Citizen, 1870 -.

Acknowledgements

The author wishes to thank Dr Norman Reid and his staff at the Department of Special Collections and Rare Books of St Andrews University, Cilla Jackson and Pam Cranston for their help in sourcing the illustrations and the university library for research facilities. Mrs E Terris, Miss F Humphries, St Andrews Preservation Trust, Lisa Wood of Fife Council Archives at Markinch, Natasha Turner of the RNLI, The Royal College of Nursing and the Commonwealth War Graves Commission.

INTRODUCTION

With the ending of hostilities in 1918, communities around the country returned, so they thought, to the world they had left in 1914 - but this was to be a different, harsher, world. St Andrews' last act of the war was the unveiling of the War Memorial, set into the wall of the cathedral's burial ground. Designed by Sir Robert Lorimer, it was unveiled by Earl Haig on 23 September 1922, and commemorated the 185 St Andrews' men who had given their lives. As a non-industrial town, St Andrews got off relatively lightly, and with the return of the golfers and summer holiday-makers in 1919, things were almost as they had been.

The 1920s brought little growth but lots of social change, thanks to the 1919 Housing, Town Planning, etc (Scotland) Act – part of David Lloyd George's 'homes for heroes' legislation - which put a duty on local authorities to clear slums and build new housing - with government subsidy if needed. In St Andrews, the town council started a new house building programme south of Kinness Burn – with Sloan Street (1922), Lamond Drive (1925), Langlands Road (1926) and Glebe Road (1927). By 1934 a total of 498 'council houses' had been completed (by 1939 this figure would rise to 762). This may have brought families out of the old, cramped and decaying town centre but, unfortunately, the town council gave little thought to preservation – demolition was the order of the day.

The spring of 1926 brought the resurrection of the student Kate Kennedy Procession, a 'right of spring' celebration, but banned in 1881 when it had become too rowdy. Originally a Victorian student, costumed, procession it was revived as a decorous historical pageant with the university's approval.

Over the period of this book, St Andrews hosted the British Open Championship on five occasions: 1921, winner (St Andrews born) Jock Hutchison (USA); 1927, Bobby Jones (USA); 1933, Denny Shute (USA); 1939, Richard Burton (England) and 1946, Sam Snead (USA). Hutchison won £75 in 1921, whilst the 2007 winner, Padraig Harrington (Ireland) lifted a purse of £750,000.

As the town moved into the 1930s, and with its population at 9,987, it felt the first effects of the Depression following the Wall Street Crash of October 1929. Compared to industrial centres, the direct effects were small - an Unemployed Men's Association was formed - but with less money in the country, fewer people could afford holidays. Growing concern at the loss of so much of the old town resulted in a public meeting in October 1937, chaired by Dr J Harry Miller, Principal of St Mary's College, where, with promised assistance from the National Trust for Scotland, St Andrews Preservation Trust was founded. What remained of old St Andrews would be protected and preserved. The Trust has played a major part in the restoration and preservation of many of the smaller historically important buildings eg; the Burgher Kirk at Imrie's Close, 136 South Street; the old house with its pend and forestair at 166-168 South Street; the 16th century building at 11 College Street; the Bogward and Kenly Green dovecotes as well as a number of other buildings. The Trust is also concerned to protect the amenities, environment and the historic character of St Andrews and its surrounding area.

The Second World War brought change, with hotels and large houses being requisitioned by the military, as the town became a training centre. Part of the West Sands was used as a training ground, and to help food production sheep grazed on the links. Another important change came on Sunday 29 June 1941 - the first Sunday golf - when the town council opened the Eden Course, a facility especially appreciated by the locally stationed military. There was no Lammas Market during the war years, but the tradition of bringing in the New Year at the Post Office followed by first-footing was maintained. By the end of the 1940s the town had around 226 shops, a mix of both family owned shops and branches of national multiples, including butchers, bakers, grocers, fishmongers, greengrocers and chemists.

The photographs which follow portray a St Andrews, just, within local memory, and it is hoped they will provide a window on the town's past, stir local memory, and supply a new view of the town for those recently come to the area.

During the period of the book students attending the university rose from a little over 1000 in 1932 to more than 2000 between 1948-51

Opposite: A view from South Street of Abbey Street before its 1969-70 widening, when all the buildings on the left, including the St Andrews Boys' Club and the Crown Hotel were demolished and not replaced. A very old street Abbey Street was first known as Prior's Wynd, then early in the 16th century it was named East Burn Wynd, and in 1843 it was re-named Abbey Street. On the right is the baker's shop of John W MacArthur – the notice in the window reads 'The shortbread Gift Shop' – We Pack and Post Daily' – which later became Roger's bakehouse and later still the St Andrews Bone China shop before closing in the 1970s. Today MacArthur's former shop remains a retail outlet having been occupied by a number of different businesses over the years. The bakehouse is now housing.

Right: The Crown Hotel stood on the east side of Abbey Street until it was demolished in December 1969, as part of the street widening programme. In the 1860s it was the Crown Inn, priding itself in its first class stabling, lock-up coach houses and large letting hall. Its last hosts were Mr and Mrs George Buchan.

Left: Before the introduction of the solid, moulded, gutta percha golf ball in 1848 golfers used 'featheries' – a leather casing packed with boiled feathers, and finished with three coats of white paint. Here James Mentiply (1883-1956), of the golf ball and club-makers Robert Forgan & Son, holds a 'feathery' and a top hat of feathers showing the quantity the ball held. Forgan's, the first to use hickory wood for their golf club shafts, was founded by Robert Forgan (1824-1900) in 1852 when he took over the business from his uncle, Hugh Philip (1782-1856) who, in 1819, had been appointed club-maker to the Society of St Andrews Golfers (from 1834, the Royal and Ancient Golf Club of St Andrews). In March 1963 the firm was taken over by A. G. Spalding of America and production relocated to Belfast. Their large premises (manufacturing and retail) ran from The Links through to Pilmuir Links, and were later occupied by the St Andrews Woollen Mill.

Opposite: St Gregory's Buildings, on the corner of Gregory's Lane and East Scores, photographed in January 1939 following a sea erosion induced landslide. Built in 1922, on the site of William Blyth's foundry (c. 1851-1920), by the masons J H White & Sons, it was gifted by Mrs Annie Younger (d. 1942), wife of Dr James Younger (1856-1946) of the Younger brewing family, of Mount Melville House, to provide modern housing for families from the decaying Ladyhead area. The Younger Graduation Hall of 1929 – opened by the future Queen Mother, Elizabeth, then Duchess of York, was built thanks to the Youngers' munificence. It was sited where some of the old fisher houses had been demolished in the Ladyhead area of North Street. Mrs Annie Younger was a generous benefactor of All Saints Episcopal Church (built 1903-1923), in North Castle Street which had originated as a fishermen's mission associated with the Episcopalian St Andrew's Church in Queen's Terrace. In its early days All Saints was known as the 'Bundle Kirk' from its practice of distributing charitable parcels. The latter's rectory was built on the site of demolished North Street fisher houses.

Restored fisher houses in the Ladyhead at 19-21 North Street. The close on the right of the building which leads to Marine Place, has the warning that cycling is prohibited. Marine Place is a quiet courtyard of houses built in 1870 for the Sea Box Society of St Andrews (1643-1920) – a friendly society for seamen. Marine Place's architect was Jesse Hall (1820-1906). To the right is the house re-modelled and renovated by James Whyte of the Abbey Bookshop in the early 1930s.

F. W. Woolworth opened this Market Street branch in April 1936, on the site of an old vernacular cottage-style house. The one-storey shop to the right was Rolland, painter and decorator, later the florist, Flowerways, and after Flowerways it became a ladies' dress shop, and was finally bought by Woolworth's for expansion.

Abbey Street, of mediaeval origin, once known as Prior's Wynd, looking towards the Co-operative premises on South Street, decorated for the Silver Jubilee of King George V on 6 May 1935. The street was a mix of houses and small businesses with Andrew Nicoll the firewood merchant and Gordon the upholsterer on the left and the Crown Hotel on the right. In company with the first Byre Theatre (1933-69) Sandy Lyall's plumbers workshop and Andrew Nicholl's premises were sited in the steading of the former Abbey Street Dairy Farm.

Miss Reid, Matron of St Andrews Memorial Cottage Hospital, kicks off a charity football match between past and present players of St Andrews United Football Club in aid of hospital funds on Thursday, 14th May 1936. The 'past' team won by five goals to two. The earliest part of the present (2008) St Andrews Memorial (Cottage) Hospital in Abbey Walk was built to a design by local architect, Charles F Anderson and opened on 27 August 1902. About half the cost of the hospital building was met from the Freddie Tait Memorial Fund, the latter a famous amateur golfer and well known in St Andrews, was killed in the Boer War in 1900 at Koodoosberg Drift. Earlier hospitals had been in rented premises at 33 Abbey Street from 1866 and Greenhill Villa (Southern Lodge) in Abbotsford Place from 1877. Rachel C M Reid came as matron in January 1904 from the Cottage Hospital at Axminster. Starting her career at St Thomas's Hospital, London, she had been a sister at both Liverpool's Hospital for Women and the Deaconess Hospital in Edinburgh. In 1914 she was seconded to the Queen Alexandria's Imperial Nursing Service, working in an operating theatre at Boulogne Casino, and was twice mentioned in dispatches. She retired from the Cottage Hospital in December 1939.

A tweed suited gentleman gazes into the window of the Abbey Bookshop at 3 South Street, opened in 1931 by the literary minded, American-born, James Whyte, who had settled in St Andrews. Whyte's hopes that his bookshop would become a literary and cultural meetingplace, barely came to fruition. Nor did his quarterly magazine, *The Modern Scot*, published between 1930 and 1936. Never quite accepted in St Andrews, he closed the shop in 1938 and returned to America. To the right, with its pillars and gates, is the entry to the 1804 built (with later additions) Priory House, with the spires of St Andrews Cathedral beyond. During the Second World War, Priory House was home to evacuees, but was demolished in 1957 and the ground returned to the curtilage of the cathedral.

The American golfer Bobby Jones (Robert Tyre Jones, 1902-1971) so loved St Andrews, and the links he first played over in 1921, that on his way to the 1936 Olympic Games in Berlin, he broke his journey to play the Old Course. Three times winner of the British Open - the latter at St Andrews in 1927 - and the British Amateur Championship in 1930, his greatest achievement was winning, in one year, 1930, the British and American Open Championships and both Amateur Championships. He was made an honorary life member of the Royal & Ancient Golf Club in 1956 and presented with the Freedom of the City Of St Andrews in October 1958. The 10th hole on the Old Course is dedicated to him.

University Principal Sir James Irvine, CBE, FRS, JP, DL, with a 'Kate' – traditionally played by a male student – and local children in Butts Wynd on a Kate Kennedy Day around 1937. Sir James (1877-1952) was Principal of the University from 1921 until his death, and although a native of Glasgow, was great lover of historic St Andrews - he received the freedom of the city in May 1930 and encouraged the founding of St Andrews Preservation Trust. Kate, the principal figure of Kate Kennedy Day is described as the niece of Bishop James Kennedy, who founded St Salvator's College in 1450.

Sorting out the 1937 Christmas mail at the Post Office in South Street. We may wonder what the parcels contained and who the lucky recipients were.

St Andrews' first picture house, the art deco, 808 seat, Cinema House on the North Street - Muttoes Lane corner, was opened in 1913 by St Andrews Cinema House Ltd. *The Scotsman* for Saturday 18 October 1913 carried the advertisement; *Wanted - Pianist (first class), lady or gentleman, for new Picture Theatre in North Street, St Andrews.* Whoever got the job, or their successor, would have been out of work in 1929 with the coming of the talkies to the Cinema House. So small was the foyer that queues for popular films would stretch up Muttoes Lane almost to Market Street. It also had a box office in Muttoes Lane for the cheapest seats. In 1947/48 seat prices ranged from 9d for the front stalls to 2/6d for the balcony. Mr Jack Humphries was the manager from 1928 until it closed in 1979. It became the 'Old Picture House', when the 936 seat 'New Picture House' - with its café and larger foyer – opened, also in North Street, in December 1930. Today (2008) the site is occupied by Muttoes Court.

The stage and auditorium of the first Byre Theatre. In 1933 local journalist and playwright Alexander B Paterson MBA, MA (1907-1989) founded the St Andrews Playing Club (from players with the theatre group of Hope Park Church), but only in 1937 did he acquire the cow byre of the old Abbey Street Dairy Farm, on a rental basis (£10 per year), from the town council. The club erected the 14 feet by 12 feet stage, installed the lighting and converted the loft to a workshop and dressing accommodation. Having acquired a public theatre licence, the first public performance in the Byre was in May 1937, when A B Paterson's one act play 'The Foreigner' was performed with Provost John Reid (1936-42) present. By the end of the season in September the actors had performed to over 1000 patrons. When the Byre was only a theatre studio the invited audiences brought their own cushions to sit on, but once the Byre opened to the public, patrons sat on the 74 tip-up seats donated by Jack Humphries of the Cinema House and so small was the auditorium that patrons were requested, by a notice, to, 'Please keep your feet off the stage'. The building was demolished in 1969, when Abbey Street was widened, and a new build 'Byre', in Abbey Street, opened the following year.

Sultan, with his 'Great War Veteran 1914-1918' medal plate - having served with the Scots Greys - and his groom John Berry in Queen's Terrace during the 1938 St Andrews Horse Parade. Later that day Berry won the special prize for most points in the gymkhana. A fine jumper and hunter, Sultan made regular appearances in the Kate Kennedy processions. He was owned by David W. Methven (born Pittenweem 1872, died at 13 Greyfriars Gardens, December 1941), proprietor of William Johnston's stables and garage at 117 Market Street and 104 - 108 North Street, which closed for area re-development in the mid 1970s. The annual horse parades, held between 1912 and 1952, were followed by gymkhanas at Cockshaugh Park, and in the age of the working horse, featured beautifully groomed horses and decorated vehicles. Sultan died in March 1939, aged 30 years.

St Andrews' last lifeboat, the *John and Sarah Hatfield* - John Hatfield and his wife Sarah of Colwyn Bay had been benefactors of the RNLI - being brought out of the lifeboat house on the East Bents in the 1930s. The 25 feet, self righting Rubie class boat – built at Thames Ironworks, Blackwall, London at a cost of £947.4/. - served from 1910 until 1938 saving at least 43 lives. In 1914 she was called out six times, saving 16 lives, including 13 from the destroyer *HMS Success*, driven ashore at Kingsbarns during a December gale. Her last coxswain, David Fenton was a fisherman and lifeboat crewman from 1898. The closure of the station and the sale of the lifeboat, less her equipment, to Valvona of Portobello as a pleasure boat, in 1938, ended a service started in 1801. The money for this 1801 lifeboat, known as 'The Cork Lifeboat' was raised by local subscription. The lifeboat house survives (2008), with a kiosk on the ground floor and St Andrews Sailing Club above. The building to the right was the Woodburn Steam Laundry Company's premises until the 1950s and is now owned by the university.

The composing room of the illustrated newspaper, the *St Andrews Times* – 'produced and printed in St Andrews by local labour' - at 122 Market Street, in July 1938. With its editorial office at 98 Market Street, it published on Wednesdays, between 1937 and 1940, as an alternative to the Cupar published St Andrews Citizen. The well known Fife journalist Tom Jarrett (1916-2005), who wrote *St Andrews Golf Links – The First 600 years* (1995) was a reporter, and George Cowie (1902-1982) contributed photographs. Between 1890 and the 1930s, the Market Street premises had been the workshop of the golf-cleek maker Robert Condie (1863-1923), whose cleek mark was a rose, and in 1986, following re-development, was named Condie Court.

A dramatic finish to a race at Madras College Sports Day in June 1938 on the University Sports Ground in Buchanan Gardens. The runners cannot be named, but standing by the tape are Mr Easson of the music department, and Mr Blue of the English department. A native of Perth and Licentiate of the Royal College of Music, 43 year old James Easson had been at Madras College since 1923 but within months of this photograph was appointed Superintendent of Music to Dundee schools. He was also the organist at the Holy Trinity Parish Church. Forty seven year old James Cameron Blue was a graduate of Glasgow University and taught at Glasgow High School before joining the staff at Madras in 1932. He died at the Cottage Hospital in September 1941.

This 1938 photograph shows a pierrot company at the Beach Pavilion, close by the Step Rock bathing pool. Afternoons and evenings they presented Scottish variety, carnival fare, request programmes, and talent-spotting competitions - with full audience participation. The terraced seating was open to wind and weather, but hardy audiences came prepared with rugs and umbrellas. In the 1950s they abandoned the Beach, staging their shows in the Town Hall, and the Pavilion became a café, and later a restaurant. The two rock formations in the water are the 'Doo-Craigs', once grass-covered haunts of pigeons. The wheeled jetty in the water, to the left of the Pavilion, was used by passengers boarding the motor boat *Ancient City*, under the captaincy of 'Commodore' James Cargill, for trips out into the Bay.

Market Street, at its junction with St Mary's Place, Bell Street and Greyfriars Garden in 1938. Its sequence of privately owned businesses and branches of national multiples included, from the left; Kermath, the chemist; (a town councillor and magistrate, William Ramsay Kermath died 15 June 1919 at St Mary's, Montrose, aged 75 years), M P Reid, children's and ladies clothier; Woolworth's; Rolland's; Crawford the baker, and Hepworth, the men's tailor. On the right is the Edinburgh based Greensmith Downes, retailer of ladies lingerie and clothing. The interspersed individual dwellinghouses, with a front door at street level and gardens, would survive complete until re-development in the 1960s.

Five to Midnight! – and revellers, with pipes and drums, have gathered outside the post office in South Street to 'bring in' the New Year - 1938. On the stroke of midnight, the bells of Holy Trinity Church (the Town Kirk) would ring out the old and ring in the new, and the traditional music and dancing, and first footing, would start. It would be a long night. The first New Year after the Second World War brought over 1,000 people onto the streets, but as the years turned into the 1950s the tradition waned as the influence of televised celebrations increased.

Going to the exhibition! A party setting off from St Andrews Railway Station in October 1938 on an excursion to the Empire Exhibition in Glasgow's Bellahouston Park. The exhibition closed on 29 October and in the last days excursions were in great demand. One such trip left St Andrews at 4.52 pm., returning after midnight - the return fare cost two shillings and sixpence. Note the boy on the right wearing a Madras College blazer and regulation navy blue and white summer socks.

As part of St Andrews' preparations for the Second World War, and the prospect of mass bombing, these men are digging the foundations of an air raid precautions shelter in South Street. At their meeting in November 1939 the town council refused to have these shelters and only acquiesced the following June.

A parade in the grounds of Madras College, thought to be the 1000 National Service Volunteers who mustered there on the evening of Wednesday, 3 May 1939, under the command of Major J Murray Prain of the Fife and Forfar Yeomanry. They were marched to the New Cinema on North Street and shown the ARP film 'The Warning' – on air raids and bombings - and afterwards addressed by Capt. A V Holt, the Territorial Army's public relations officer in Fife.

A War Weapons Week parade marching along South Street. Opposite, (from right to left), are the shop premises of John Lang, the draper and clothier, (later Fred Mackenzie, ironmonger); the Central Café; and William Birrell, wine merchant and grocer. South Street's first lime trees were planted in 1879 on the north side of the street, thanks to John Milne (1823-1904), architect and town councillor. 1880 saw limes planted on the south side of the street.

Members of the Women's Voluntary Service march along South Street as part of a wartime parade, their placard reading – WVS *Knitting For Sailors, Kilrule Depot*, and followed by a YMCA van. Formed in 1938, the WVS fulfilled many necessary, and practical, wartime jobs including work in hospitals and children's nurseries, tending to air raid victims and running and staffing canteens, including mobile ones. To the left of the banner is 'Keith the Chemist', later taken over by T M McKechnie - both well-known St Andreans. A collection of period dispensing items from the shop is now on display at the St Andrews Preservation Trust Museum in North Street.

To encourage National Savings and hence help the war effort there were, across the country, many *Wings For Victory, Warship* and *War Weapons weeks*. This photograph of a 1942 *Warship Week* parade in South Street shows a 25 pounder field gun (capable of firing its 87mm, 11.3kg shell a distance of 12,250 metres) being towed by a Polish Army armoured car. In the background is Cowie & Govan's photographic shop, the Art Needlework Shop (2008 - Carlton Bakeries), the main post office and the long-established and well-remembered Mrs Taylor's Ladies Outfitters (2008 – M&Co. - the clothing and household linen retailer).

University Principal Sir James Irvine meeting General Wladyslaw Sikorski, Commander-in-Chief of the Polish forces in Britain, in South Street in September 1941. Born in Galicia, then part of the Austro-Hungarian Empire, in 1881 Sikorski became Polish Prime Minister in exile in September 1939. Returning from an inspection tour of Polish forces in the Middle East in July 1943 he was killed when his aircraft crashed on take-off from Gibraltar. An honorary degree was conferred on General Sikorsky by St Andrews University, and a memorial to the general is in Kinburn Park.

'Number Sixty' South Street during the Second World War. The signs outside, in English, Dutch and Polish reads; *'Number Sixty - Reading, Writing and Recreation Rooms for Men in H M Forces. Open 2.30pm to 10pm'*. The many servicemen stationed in and around St Andrews appreciated its comforts and facilities. There was also a servicewomen's club and hostel at 7 Howard Place, with local volunteers running both.

Prime Minister Winston Churchill inspecting St Andrew's coastal defences and the Polish forces manning them on Wednesday 23 October 1940. Also in the photograph are Mrs Churchill and General Wladyslaw Sikorski of the Polish forces. Turbans, as worn by Mrs Churchill, were a wartime fashion.

Three St Andrews children in their, thick, wool half-hose and stockings, passing the Volunteer Hall in Alexandra Place, with their newly issued gas masks in regulation cardboard boxes – gas mask practices took place in schools during the war. Thirty-eight million were issued throughout Britain – but never used. Distribution in East Fife began at Anstruther, reaching St Andrews in the second week of March 1939. Later, canvas or rexine bags, with shoulder straps, were used to protect the gasmask cardboard boxes from wear and tear.

Evacuees, all neatly labelled and carrying their gas masks, arriving in St Andrews. The first batch came on 2 September 1939 and the second, bringing the total to 350, two weeks later. There were sufficient families in St Andrews to take the children – indeed St Andrews led the way in Fife – but the greatest problem for the Chief Reception Officer, Mr J Cargill Cantley, was their education. The infants went to the West Infant School, the juniors to the East End School, or Fisher School, and the senior and post primary to the Burgh School and Madras College. These children were, apparently, from Edinburgh but there were also children from London, Glasgow and Dunfermline who stayed with relatives.

Left: Wartime ephemera with advice and guidance on rationing, evacuation, economising on fuel and, the Home Guard Handbook (Hodder & Stoughton, 1942) by. John Brophy (1899-1965), the left wing Liverpudlian novelist and journalist.

Opposite: Civilian gas masks came in three sizes - small, medium and large - and the model for babies, here being demonstrated to mothers. A model for the elderly was operated by a hand-bellows. Fortunately, they would never be used.

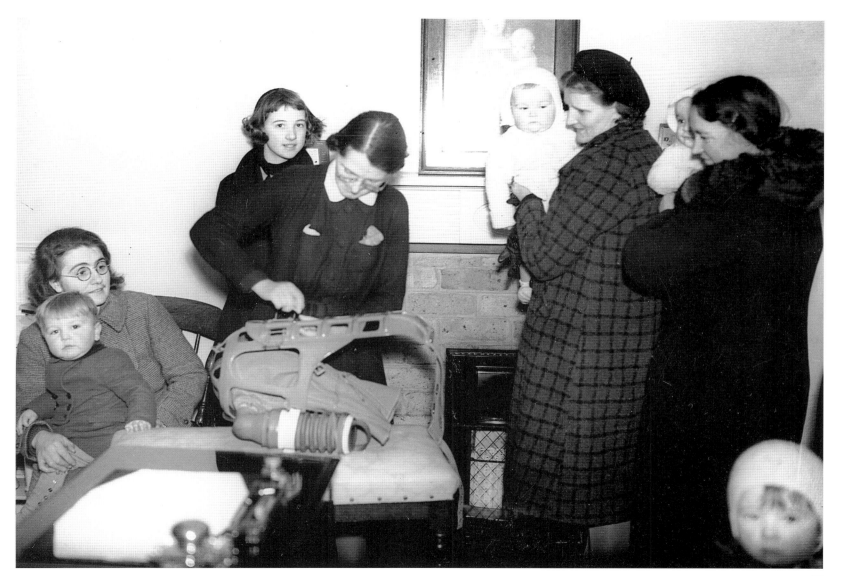

Soldiers on the West Sands filling sandbags to protect the town's important buildings, including the post office in South Street.

Despite the barbed wire, as here at the Step Rock, the anti tank blocks and the wooden stakes on the west sands to impale enemy paratroopers, St Andrews remained a popular holiday resort throughout the war.

The wartime air raid siren was atop Kinburn House, in the park, and first heard on 20 October 1939. The town was first bombed on the evening of 25 October 1940 when this house, 'White Cottage' on Greenside Place near to Kinnessburn Road was struck by the second in a stick of four bombs. The first landed in the Kinness Burn. The third bomb fell at the south end of Westburn Lane damaging the university's Bute Medical Building, while the fourth bomb exploded in the quadrangle of St Mary's College, badly damaging the Carnegie extension of the university library. The cottage, empty at the time, was home to Mrs Annie Brand, the 81 year old widow of James Brand, a retired engine driver, who had died in March 1938, aged 83 years. Mrs Brand died in January 1944.

On Thursday 6 August 1942, a lone German bomber, possibly returning from a raid over Dundee, jettisoned its bombs south of the Kinness Burn, striking this semi-detached house, 'Almar' and 'Dunusan' in Nelson Street. Due to a power failure, there had been no air raid warning. Albert Alfred Brown (45) died in the rubble of his home, Almar, whilst the following died in Dunusan: 64 year old Susan Adair Chalmers, the house owner; Margaret McDonald (48), an air raid warden from Rutherglen with her daughters, Mary Watson McDonald (22) and Dorothy Beth McDonald (17); James Wood (42) of Hazel Drive, Dundee, his 40 year old wife Helen Cobban Wood, and their daughters Helen (15) and Avril (9), with Mrs Woods 77 year old mother, Helen Ross Welsh. An air raid warden, 58 year old William Wilson, of Wilson's Garage died the following day of injuries sustained when he was struck by a falling stone in the attempted rescue. Houses in nearby Park Street were also badly damaged.

General Dwight David Eisenhower, Supreme Commander of Allied Forces during the invasion of Europe in 1944 and future two-term President of the United States of America, at St Andrews in October 1946 when he was granted honorary life membership of the Royal and Ancient Golf Club. Pictured with him is Roger Wethered (1899-1983), Captain of the R & A. Eisenhower chose to walk the first hole – 'I don't mind disgracing myself before all these spectators, but if I missed the ball, my staff would never forgive me' - and played 13 others, accompanied by club professional Willie Auchterlonie and Bob Henrit who carried for him.

The scoreboard at the 1946 British Open Championship when, watched by a crowd of 12,000, the American Sam Snead (1912-2002) won by four strokes. The bandstand, to the left of the board, was manufactured at Walter MacFarlane's Saracen Foundry in Glasgow and erected in by the town council 1905. This area of the Butts – used in times past for archery practice –is still a favourite Sunday walk for many families.

The 17th tee on the Old Course, possibly during the 1946 British Open Golf Championship with a player just having tee-ed off. In the distance is the wooden bridge across the St Andrews - Leuchars railway line which once bisected the Eden Course until the line's closure in 1969.

The golf professional David Ayton (1882-1963) with a children's class in the summer of 1948. He and his brother Lawrence B Ayton were sons of the St Andrews born professional, David Ayton, and both followed his footsteps. From 1911, after experimental work with golf balls in London, David started a successful career as a professional player and coach in Britain, America and Canada. In St Andrews, he taught the Children's Golf Club and St Leonard's School for fifteen years, and was the official coach at HMS Cochrane, the naval establishment at Donibristle. He had also been a champion swimmer and was a founder member of the 1st St Andrews Boys Brigade. The Ayton family had an unbroken connection with St Andrews Golf Club from its formation in 1843 and an ancestor is said to have served with Nelson on *HMS Victory* at the Battle of Trafalgar.

The dining room of the six-storey, red Dumfries sandstone, Grand Hotel (opened 1896) in the late 1940s. During the war it had been requisitioned by, as can be guessed by the paintings, the Royal Air Force. In January 1950 it became the university's Hamilton Hall, a hostel accommodating 100 male students in 78 rooms.

The South Street – Queens Gardens junction in 1949 with the Town Hall on the left and the Bank of Scotland building on the right. The Town Hall, incorporating the police station, opened in 1861 and succeeded the centuries old Town House, with its adjoining prison, the Tolbooth in Market Street – its site now marked with coloured setts. The 1695 founded Bank of Scotland came to St Andrews in 1792, when its agent was Charles Dempster and his son Cathcart, working from an office in Westburn Lane. The bank building in this photograph went up in 1871 and was re-built in 1960. In the foreground the pink, polished, Peterhead granite drinking fountain – now in Kinburn Park – was raised to the memory of Major-General Robert S Baden-Powell and his men for their bravery in holding Mafeking during the Boer War (1899-1902).